D0722834

For the girls, Gloria and Wilma
CC

With thanks to my family—
Mum, Dad, and Matt; Simon H B,
Lilia, Iris, and Neve
LD

First US edition 2021

Library of Congress Catalog Card Number pending
ISBN 978-1-5362-2036-0

21 22 23 24 25 26 TLF 10 9 8 7 6 5 4 3 2 1

Printed in Dongguan, Guangdong, China

This book was typeset in IM FELL DW Pica and Neucha.
The illustrations were done in watercolor, gouache, and
colored pencil.

Candlewick Press
99 Dover Street
Somerville, Massachusetts 02144

www.candlewick.com

WOMBAT

CHRISTOPHER CHENG

ILLUSTRATED BY LIZ DUTHIE

CANDLEWICK PRESS

Far underground, where dirt and tree roots mesh, tunnels lead to a burrow. There, Wombat's day begins. She ventures outside, alert and hungry, as a fading sun says farewell to the day.

Wombats are nocturnal marsupials and spend most of the daytime in burrows.

1

She grinds nearby grasses for a perfect breakfast feast.

With a satisfied stomach, she ambles along her well-worn path.

She stops to dig, but the ground collapses. Too soft!

So Wombat wanders again, searching for a better place to dig.

Wombats have four large incisor teeth (two on the top, two on the bottom) for cutting and molars and premolars for grinding. The teeth have no roots. They never stop growing.

Wombats' broad, flat heads, barrel-shaped bodies, powerful shoulders, and short legs with flat, clawed feet make them perfect diggers. They can burrow 3 feet (1 meter) in a night.

What's this?
A fence is blocking her journey.
That doesn't stop this determined
wombat—the bulldozer of the bush.
She starts digging rhythmically.

Left foot, left foot.
Right foot, right foot.
Again and again.
Under she goes, and soon she
appears on the other side.
A good shake and scratch
will clean her fur.

Near a rotting tree, Wombat continues
digging and ripping,
pushing and shoveling.
Back through the tunnel she shuffles,
moving the dirt outside.

This long tunnel will join a burrow
lined with grasses and leaves—
a perfect place for sleeping.
But much more excavating is needed.

*Wombats use their strong
front limbs for digging. They use their
front and back limbs to push the dirt out
of the tunnel. They might even roll onto
their side to dig out the walls and
roof of a burrow.*

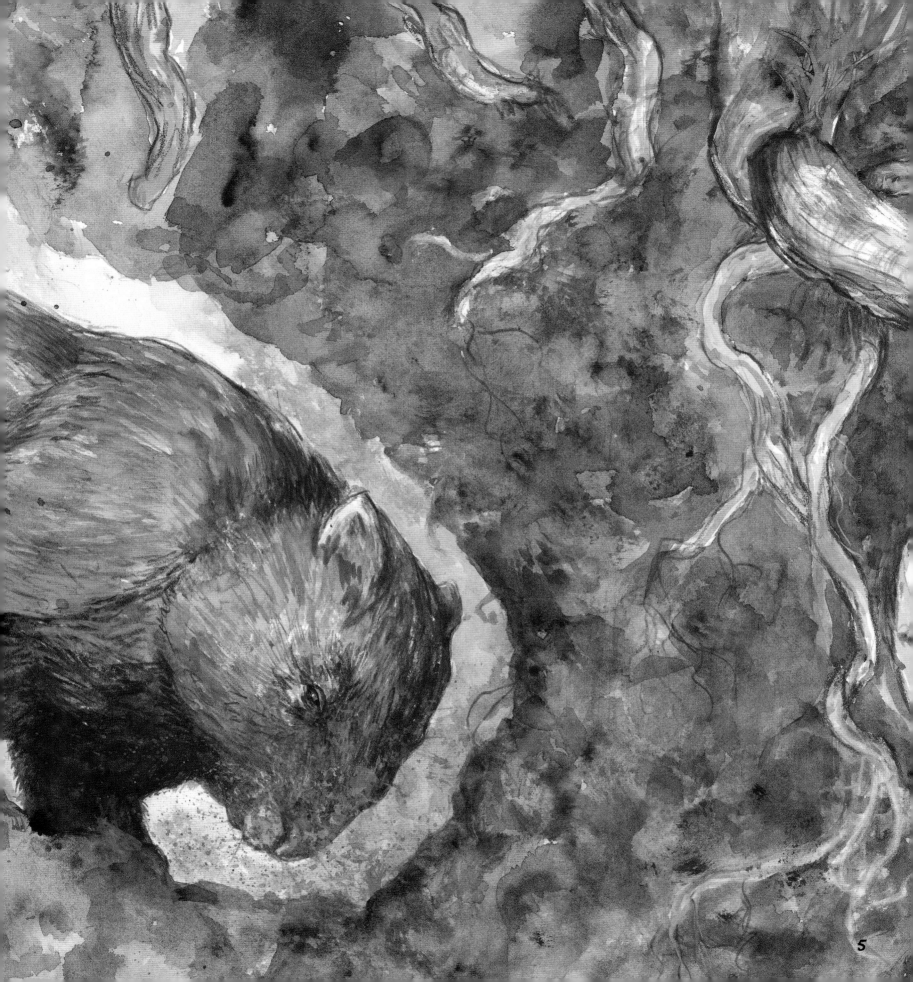

When the sun is high in the sky, the heat is intense. Even galahs stop their raucous antics.

Now is when Wombat must sleep. Another wombat might share her cool burrow. Wombat doesn't mind—this time.

Burrows help wombats stay cool in summer and warm in winter, protected from the elements—and safe from predators. Wombats have many burrows. A major burrow can be up to 11½ feet (3.5 meters) deep and almost 100 feet (30 meters) long. Generations of wombats may have used this burrow. Wombats might share burrows for resting, but they usually won't share feeding areas.

The next day as she explores, Wombat rubs her body against a worn spot on a tree and leaves her cube-shaped poop on a rock. Other forest dwellers need to be reminded that this is her territory.

Wombats have some of the driest poop of any mammal. This helps them to conserve water.

Wombat sniffs.
A strange smell wafts through the air.
It doesn't smell like the dappled forest.
It smells like WOMBAT!

A younger wombat is in her territory. This intruder is not allowed here.

Wombats have a keen sense of hearing and a strong sense of smell, perfect for detecting danger. If needed, they can run very quickly for a short distance— up to 25 miles (40 kilometers) per hour.

Wombat snarls.
The stranger looks up,
then goes on eating.
Wombat screeches.
The stranger pauses.
Wombat charges!

This time the intruder runs.
Wombat snorts loudly,
a final warning to remind
the stranger who lives here.

*Wombats have poor eyesight. Their ears are short,
slightly rounded, and small. Their button-like noses with
nostrils at the tip are hairless and covered in grainy skin.
They have coarse, thick fur, a bit like a doormat.*

A shaft of sunlight pierces the forest canopy.
The forest floor is a perfect place for a conquering wombat
to bask on her back and warm her stomach!

Wombat senses another intruder.
The land is alive with animals.
Most don't worry Wombat,
but Dingo is a predator she fears.

She sniffs.
She listens.
She waits.

Stealthily,
Dingo approaches,
step by step.

*Common wombats don't have many
natural predators, although wild dogs
and foxes are a danger. The biggest
threat to their survival is the loss of
habitat through land clearing.*

13

Danger!

Wombat runs.
Dingo chases.
Wombat passes a fallen
branch—no shelter there.
And there is no sanctuary at
a collapsed tunnel entrance.

Jaws wide open,
Dingo pounces.

Injured wombats will cover
their wounds with dirt to
allow them to heal.

Safety!
Wombat dives into a
nearby tunnel.
She feels Dingo's
hot breath as she
squeezes inside.

She stops.

Dingo pants, sniffing at the entrance, waiting.
Wombat stands firm, her bony bottom blocking the way!
Dingo scratches Wombat, but she doesn't flinch.

16

A wombat's thick-skinned, bony bottom could crush a predator's skull against the tight burrow entrance.

Defeated, Dingo leaves.
He won't catch Wombat today.

17

Wombat is tired, but the old chamber
at the end of this tunnel is crowded.
She chooses another place
where she can be alone.

A secret is
snug in her
pouch.

A female wombat is pregnant for approximately thirty days.
The newborn will weigh about a third of an ounce (1 gram) at
birth, looking like a pink jelly bean. Measuring just over an inch
(3 centimeters), it is about the size of a child's little finger.

Female wombats have a backward-facing pouch. This keeps it
from filling with dirt while she is digging. It also protects the
young. The pouch is almost hairless.

As night returns, the nocturnal
chorus greets the darkening day,
and so will Wombat.
She cautiously peers outside,
her wary joey nuzzled beside her.

*Wombats have whiskers above the eyes,
on the cheeks, under the chin, and near the
throat, but the most sensitive whiskers are
around the nose. Wombats have a very small
tail, which is hidden by fur.*

20

He looks and scratches.
He digs and munches.
Sniffing and wandering,
next to his mother,
he learns the wombat ways.

Information About Wombats

A group of wombats is called a colony or a wisdom—although you won't often find them together! Most common wombats like the solitary life. Wombats can survive for a long time without drinking any water. Most of their moisture comes from the plants they eat. Each night, wombats spend between three and eight hours grazing on native grasses and herbs and eating roots, traveling a mile or more and visiting burrows. After gestation, the young wombat crawls about 4 inches (10 centimeters) from the birth canal to the female's backward-facing pouch and attaches to one of her two teats. For at least six months after birth, wombats develop in the pouch. Then they remain with their mother for at least eight more months, eating plants and still drinking some milk. They usually stop suckling at one year of age.

INDEX

Look up the pages to find out about these wombat things.

Don't forget to look at both kinds of words—
this kind and *this kind.*

CHRISTOPHER CHENG is the author of *Python*, illustrated by Mark Jackson. He established the Zoomobile at Taronga Zoo in Sydney, Australia, and also taught at the zoo for eight years. He is now a full-time award-winning author of children's books of many genres. He lives in Sydney in a home filled with picture books.

LIZ DUTHIE is an artist and the education officer at the La Trobe Art Institute, Bendigo. She is passionate about nature and bringing native creatures to life. Liz Duthie lives in Australia.